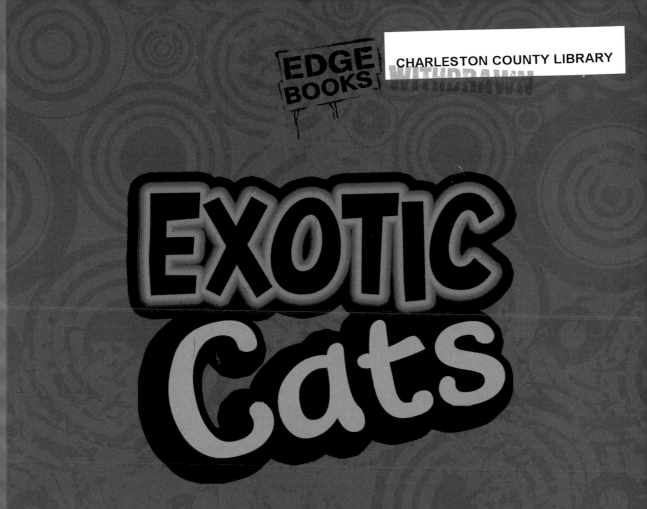

EXOTIC
Cats

by Joanne Mattern

CAPSTONE PRESS
a capstone imprint

Edge Books are published by Capstone Press,
1710 Roe Crest Drive, North Mankato, Minnesota 56003
www.capstonepub.com

Books published by Capstone Press are manufactured with paper
containing at least 10 percent post-consumer waste.

Library of Congress Cataloging-in-Publication Data
Mattern, Joanne, 1963–
   Exotic cats / by Joanne Mattern.
      p. cm.—(Edge books. all about cats)
   Includes bibliographical references and index.
   Summary: "Describes the history, physical features, temperament,
      and care of the Exotic cat breed"—Provided by publisher.
   ISBN 978-1-4296-6630-5 (library binding)
   1. Exotic shorthair cat—Juvenile literature. I. Title. II. Series.
   SF449.E93M383 2011
   636.8'2—dc22   2010037844

Editorial Credits
Connie R. Colwell and Anthony Wacholtz, editors; Heidi Thompson, designer;
   Wanda Winch, media researcher; Eric Manske, production specialist

Photo Credits
Alamy: Juniors bildarchiv, 9, 14; Photo by Fiona Green, 17, 21, 23, 26, 29, Fiona
Green/Silver 'N Gold Cattery, Texas, 6, 19, 25; Shutterstock: Eric Isselée, cover,
Linn Currie, 16, PozitivStudija, 5, 15, Tamila Aspen (TAStudio), 11, Vasiliy
Khimenko, 13

Printed in the United States of America in Stevens Point, Wisconsin.
052012   006735R

TABLE OF CONTENTS

Chapter 1

TEDDY BEAR CATS

With a flat face, snub nose, and short fur, Exotics are easy cats to spot. Their appearance has led to the nickname "teddy bear" cats. The nickname fits in well with their personalities too. Exotics are friendly, affectionate cats. They like to be around people. Exotics make great family pets and are known for their cleanliness. They are also good for families with busy lifestyles. Although they enjoy companionship, they are known to be independent cats sometimes. If they do want attention, they won't be shy. They may climb into your lap while you're reading or follow you from room to room.

In 2009 Exotics were ranked the second most popular **breed** according to the Cat Fanciers' Association (CFA). Exotics placed only behind their longhaired cousins, Persians. The CFA is the world's largest cat **registry**.

breed—a certain kind of animal within an animal group; breed also means to mate and raise a certain kind of animal

registry—an organization that keeps track of the ancestry for cats of a certain breed

With their sweet expression and teddy-bear look, Exotics are one of the most popular cat breeds.

IS AN EXOTIC RIGHT FOR YOU?

Exotics have a good balance in their personalities. They are affectionate and fun-loving, but they like to be alone sometimes. These traits make Exotics the perfect choice for families who are away from the house often. Exotics are also a popular breed because they have short hair and don't shed as much as some other cats.

Exotics enjoy getting attention from their owners.

People who are interested in owning an Exotic cat can look for one in several ways. They may contact animal shelters, breed rescue organizations, or breeders. Animal shelters or rescue organizations can be less expensive places to purchase an Exotic cat. You can find information about breed rescue organizations by heading to the computer. Rescue organizations often have their own Internet sites. They may also advertise in newspapers or cat magazines. Some rescue organizations specialize in finding homes for Exotics. The cats are usually adults and may even be registered.

Exotics from breeders can cost several hundred dollars. But there is an added benefit from buying an Exotic from a breeder. Breeders often know the cat's parents and medical history. Responsible breeders take extra steps to make sure the cats will be healthy when people take them home. Cats sometimes inherit diseases from their parents. Responsible cat breeders test their animals for diseases. They will not breed animals that suffer from serious illnesses. If you don't buy your cat from a breeder, be sure to ask about the cat's medical history.

trait—a quality or characteristic that makes one person or animal different from another

inherit—to receive a characteristic from parents

Chapter 2

EXOTIC HISTORY

American Shorthair breeders developed the Exotic cat in the 1960s. American Shorthairs are medium-sized cats with short fur. Some breeders wanted their cats to have silver coats. Because some Persians had silver coats, breeders began crossing American Shorthairs with Persians.

Some of the resulting kittens had the desired silver coats. But they did not look like American Shorthairs. The kittens had short, plush coats, and their faces looked like those of Persians. Breeders became interested in these unique-looking cats with short coats. They began to cross Persians with other shorthaired cats such as Russian Blues and Burmese.

In 1966 the CFA accepted the new mixed breed as a separate breed. This breed was called the Exotic Shorthair. Later the name was changed to Exotic.

FACT: Sterling was another name considered for the Exotic breed because of the silver hair of the first cats.

The Exotic breed was created accidentally. The cats had a similar appearance to Persians but the coat length of American Shorthairs.

Over the next 20 years, the CFA's Exotic breed standard changed often. In 1987 breeders decided that Exotics could only be crossbred with Persians.

Three years later, breeders came up with a simple way to describe the Exotic breed standard. Because an Exotic looks like a Persian cat, breeders thought the two breeds should have similar standards. Breeders decided that any future change made to the Persian standard would be made for the Exotic standard as well.

MODERN APPEARANCE

Because of the breed standard changes, today's Exotic cats look more like Persians than Exotics of the past. The only difference between Exotics and Persians is the length of the Exotic's coat. Modern breeders develop Exotics by crossing Persians with shorthaired cats. But breeders do this only once. The breeders then take the kittens from these matches and breed them with Persians. That's why modern Exotic kittens are almost entirely Persian. Exotics are very similar to Persians in both appearance and personality.

breed standard—certain physical features in a breed that judges look for at a cat show

crossbreed—to mix one breed with another breed

Persian

Chapter 3

THE EXOTIC LOOK

Exotics are medium-sized cats. Adult Exotics weigh between 8 and 15 pounds (3.6 and 6.8 kilograms). Their bodies are stocky and low to the ground. They have short, sturdy legs. Their paws are large and round, and their tails are short and thick.

COATS

Exotics have short, plush coats made up of thick, soft fur. The fur does not tangle or mat as easily as the fur of a Persian cat. Exotics have a double coat. Thick, soft hair lies close to the skin. The thick layer of fur is covered by lighter, coarse fur.

Exotic cats have short hair because of their **genes**. Genes determine a cat's coat type, color, and gender. Kittens receive a pair of genes for each trait. They receive one gene from their mother and one gene from their father.

The gene for a shorthaired coat is dominant. Dominant genes are stronger than other genes. Cats with short coats need only one gene for short hair.

gene—the part of a cell that carries information about how a living thing will look and behave

12

Exotic kittens look like Persian kittens but have shorter coats.

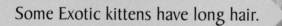

Some Exotic kittens have long hair.

These genes can make it difficult to breed Exotic cats. Exotic kittens sometimes inherit one gene for long hair from each parent. These kittens will have long hair. They will look like Persians, but they are still considered to be Exotics. Some breed organizations recognize these cats as a different breed, the Exotic Longhair.

FACIAL FEATURES

Exotics have unique faces that are only shared with Persian cats. Both breeds have snub noses and flat faces. But the fur on an Exotic's face is much shorter than the fur on a Persian's face.

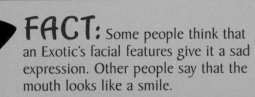

FACT: Some people think that an Exotic's facial features give it a sad expression. Other people say that the mouth looks like a smile.

COLORS

Exotics can be many colors. The most common Exotic colors are black, tortoiseshell, red tabby, brown tabby, and bi-color. Tortoiseshell Exotics are covered in patches of red, black, and cream fur. Tabby Exotics' coats are mixed with dark, striped markings. Bi-color Exotics have coats with patches of white and another color. These colors include black, cream, red, tabby, or blue. Blue Exotics have blue-gray coats.

Some Exotics have solid white coats.

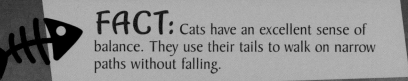

FACT: Cats have an excellent sense of balance. They use their tails to walk on narrow paths without falling.

Exotics like to play with toys they can chew on or chase.

PERSONALITY

Exotics make excellent pets. They are known for their friendly and easygoing personalities. They get along well with dogs, children, and other cats. Exotics are playful but gentle cats. They like attention and often follow their owners from room to room. Some breeders say male Exotics tend to be more affectionate than females.

Chapter 4

CARING FOR AN EXOTIC

Exotics are strong, healthy cats. They can live 15 years or more with good care. Like other cats, Exotics should be kept indoors. Outdoor cats are at a much greater risk of developing diseases. They also are exposed to dangers such as cars and other animals.

FEEDING

Exotic cats need high-quality food. Most pet foods available in supermarkets or pet stores provide a balanced, healthy diet.

You have some options for what to feed your cat. You could give your cat dry food. This food is usually the least expensive type of cat food. It will not spoil if it is left in a dish.

You could also give your cat moist, canned food. This type of food should not be left out for more than one hour. It will spoil if it is left out for long periods of time.

Dry food can help keep Exotic cats' teeth clean.

19

Different cats may prefer different types of food. Ask your veterinarian for advice on which type of food is best for your cat.

Cats need to drink water to stay healthy. You should keep your cat's bowl filled with fresh, clean water. Be sure to dump out the water and refill the bowl each day. Although cats like the taste of milk, you shouldn't allow an adult cat to drink it. Adult cats can have trouble digesting milk.

NAIL CARE

Exotic cats need their nails trimmed each month. Trimming helps reduce damage if cats scratch the carpet or furniture. It also protects cats from infections caused by ingrown nails. Infections can occur when a cat does not sharpen its claws often enough. The nails then grow into the bottom of the paw.

It is best to begin trimming a cat's nails when it is a kitten. The kitten will become used to having its nails trimmed as it grows older. Ask your veterinarian how to trim your cat's nails.

FACT: Cats can retract, or draw back in, their nails when they aren't using them to keep the claws sharp.

DENTAL CARE

Exotic cats also need regular dental care to protect their teeth and gums from plaque. You should brush your cat's teeth at least once each week. Use a special toothbrush made for cats or a soft cloth. You should never use toothpaste made for people to brush your cat's teeth. Cats may become sick if they swallow it. Use a toothpaste made especially for cats.

When brushing your Exotic's teeth, use one arm to keep your cat from moving.

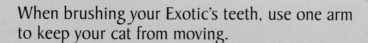

plaque—the coating of food, saliva, and bacteria that forms on teeth and can cause tooth decay

LITTER BOXES

You will need to provide a **litter** box for your Exotic cat. Cats get rid of bodily waste in litter boxes. The litter should be 2 to 3 inches (5 to 7.6 centimeters) deep. Different types of cat litter can be purchased at pet supply stores or supermarkets. Most litter is made of clay, but some is made of wood, wheat, or corn. Remember to clean the waste out of the box each day. You should also change the litter at least once every two weeks. Cats are clean animals and may refuse to use a dirty litter box.

FACT: Your cat may not use the litter box if it is placed too close to its food and water.

litter—small bits of clay or other material used to absorb the waste of cats and other animals

A litter box should have enough room for your cat to move around and easily get in and out.

COAT GROOMING

Most cats do a good job of grooming their fur with their tongues. But sometimes an Exotic needs help from its owner. Their coat grows very thick in the winter. In late spring, Exotics begin to lose this thick coat. In spring and summer, Exotics should be combed more often than they are in the winter and fall. Combing removes loose hair, prevents mats, and keeps the coat shiny.

You should comb your Exotic with a fine-toothed metal comb each week. Be gentle as you comb. If you comb too hard, pieces off fur can break off. You could also scrape your cat's skin.

If your cat's fur does mat, you should never use scissors to cut out the mats. You could damage the coat or cut your cat's skin. Instead, have a professional groomer remove mats.

Exotics sometimes develop dark stains around their eyes. Tears easily leak out of Exotics' large eyes and down their flat faces. These tears contain bacteria that can stain Exotics' fur. You should clean around your cat's eyes every day with a moistened tissue or cloth.

You can use a cotton swab to gently clean around your Exotic's eyes.

Proper health care for Exotics includes regular grooming.

 **FACT:** Cats can hear sounds that humans cannot hear. Cats can also see better in the dark than people.

HEALTH CARE

Exotic cats must visit a veterinarian regularly for checkups. Vets will check the cat's heart, eyes, ears, mouth, and coat. Most vets recommend yearly visits for cats. Older cats may need to visit the vet two or three times each year. Cats tend to have more health problems as they get older. More frequent checkups help vets treat these health problems early.

At the first check-up, ask the vet about which vaccinations your cat needs. Cats should receive vaccinations to protect against diseases such as rabies and feline leukemia. Cats can also be vaccinated against several respiratory diseases that cause breathing or lung problems.

vaccination—a shot of medicine that protects animals from a disease

Owners who are not planning to breed their cats should have them spayed or neutered. Veterinarians perform these surgeries. Spaying and neutering animals makes it impossible for them to breed. The surgeries help control the pet population. They also help keep your cat from getting certain infections and diseases. Spayed and neutered cats usually have calmer personalities than cats that are not spayed or neutered. They also are unlikely to wander away from home to find mates.

Cats lick themselves to groom their coats and stay clean. They often swallow loose pieces of fur. This fur can then form into hairballs in the cat's stomach. The only way the cat can get rid of hairballs is to vomit them up. Large hairballs can get stuck in the cat's digestive system. Surgery may be needed to remove them. The best way to prevent hairballs is to comb your Exotic regularly.

The playful attitude and easygoing nature of Exotics make them family favorites. By taking good care of your "teddy bear" cat, you can help your quiet companion be at your side for many years.

With proper care, an Exotic can live a long, healthy life with your family.

GLOSSARY

breed (BREED)—a certain kind of animal within an animal group; breed also means to mate and raise a certain kind of animal

breed standard (BREED STAN-durd)—certain physical features in a breed that judges look for at a cat show

crossbreed (KRAWSS-breed)—to mix one breed with another breed

gene (JEEN)—the part of a cell that carries information about how a living thing will look and behave

hairball (HAIR-bawl)—a ball of fur that lodges in a cat's stomach

inherit (in-HAIR-it)—to receive a characteristic from a parent

litter (LIT-ur)—small bits of clay or other material used to absorb the waste of cats and other animals

plaque (PLAK)—the coating of food, saliva, and bacteria that forms on teeth and can cause tooth decay

registry (REH-juh-stree)—an organization that keeps track of the ancestry for cats of a certain breed

trait (TRATE)—a quality or characteristic that makes one person or animal different from another

vaccination (vak-suh-NAY-shun)—a shot of medicine that protects animals from a disease

READ MORE

Jenkins, Steve. *Dogs and Cats*. Boston: Houghton Mifflin Co., 2007.

Rau, Dana Meachen. *Top 10 Cats for Kids*. Top Pets for Kids with American Humane. Berkeley Heights, N.J.: Enslow Elementary, 2009.

Stone, Lynn M. *Exotic Cats*. Eye to Eye With Cats. Vero Beach, Fla.: Rourke Pub., 2010.

INTERNET SITES

FactHound offers a safe, fun way to find Internet sites related to this book. All of the sites on FactHound have been researched by our staff.

Here's all you do:

Visit *www.facthound.com*

Type in this code: 9781429666305

Super-cool stuff! Check out projects, games and lots more at **www.capstonekids.com**

INDEX